CONTENTS

Publisher's Note	3
Peace	6
Creating an Economic Environment in South Sudan That Will Work	8
Rethinking Wealth as South Sudan Develops	12
Water and the Future of South Sudan	18
A Conversation with Paramount Chief Dr. Abuk Deng Mashama Angui	26
A Conversation with Achuei Deng Ajing	31
The Pride of South Sudan	32
Can Sudan Survive?	36
Kenya's Elections	37
Akon Esther	38
A Dinka Man's Fight for the Existence of His Language Abroad	40
Why the Kiir Administration Should Tap into South Sudanese Diaspora's Expertise	42
My Culture is My Identity	44
Back to His Roots	46
TWIC East Leaders In Australia Encourage Children To Learn Dinka Language	48
Aduk Gideon Dau, the Jonglei Daughter Educating Vulnerable Children in Kenya	51
TWIC East Community Leaders Doing Wonders in Western Australia	54
Book Reviews	57

Our Staff:
Publisher: Deng Mayik Atem, USA
Editor in Chief: Kenneth Weene, USA
Senior Editor: Christy White, USA

Staff Writers:
Asara Bullen Panchol-Juba, South Sudan
Adhieu Majok, London

Contributing Writer: Adut Bior, Kampala, Uganda

Photographers:
Tino Matoc Deng Mangok, Turalei, Warrap State
Mustafa Khan-Juba, South Sudan
Dani' Lee-Juba, South Sudan
K Peas Cuts, Juba, South Sudan
Adja, Juba, South Sudan

Board of Directors:
David Dau Acuoth-Juba, South Sudan
Francis Buk-Juba, South Sudan
Bol Madut Bol, Juba, South Sudan
Peter Lual Deng –Australia
Martin G. Abucha-Juba, South Sudan
Asara Bullen, Juba, South Sudan

Executives:
Deng Mayik Atem-CEO/President
Gabriel Mabeny Kuot-CFO
Atong Guot Mayol: Director of Public Relations
Anger Madut Ayii: Creative Designer
Adhar Dor Mayar- Marketing director
Awien Rose-Kampala, Uganda

Editorial Offices:
Phoenix, AZ United States
Contact: 1.602-348-2650
Juba, South Sudan
Contact: +21197731641
www.ramcielmagazine.com
info@ramcielmagazine.com

ISBN: 9780645819571

Cover design by Monykuer
Typesetting and layout by Africa World Books
Unit 3, 57 Frobisher St, Osborne Park, WA 6017
P.O. Box 1106 Osborne Park, WA 6916

WELCOME

-- PUBLISHER'S NOTE --

Dear Readers:

According to world politics South Sudan exists as a nation. For example, our flag flies in front of the United Nations headquarters along with those of 192 other countries. If you use Google or some other search engine, you can learn that Juba is South Sudan's capital and that our motherland is composed of ten states. There it is, the reality we call South Sudan.

But is South Sudan really a nation, or is it an accident of British Empire building and a European notion of geography? Let's start with Juba. Were you going to pick the location of a capital for our country, would it not be better to be in the north, closer to the center of the nation? The British were not interested in founding a capital for what was eventually to become our motherland; they wanted to control the White Nile. But to this day, there are many who say that a new capital should be built - Ramciel.

Beyond the location of Juba, what do states have to do with our country? We are a nation of tribal identities not geographic locations. By basing our government elections on geography, the constitution gives the larger tribes disproportionate power in decision-making and it deprives us of what should be an emphasis on shared values and faiths. In this issue Ramciel is proud to begin a dialog about the role of traditional tribal structures and beliefs with our interview of Sultana Abuk Macham Angui. In the future, we need to encourage more discussion among tribal leaders and religious figures to find those values and beliefs that will highlight our peoples and our traditions.

One of the best South Sudanese traditions is our love of music and dance. Even though we may not all sing in the same language or dance the same steps, we can share and enjoy one with the other. One of the most popular musicians among us—both those of us at home and those living in the

Diaspora—is Achuei Deng Ajing. Miss Achuei recently toured the United States and brought a touch of home to those of us living in America. As publisher of Ramciel I am delighted to share our interview with Achuei Deng Ajing.

While music has always been an integral part of life for South Sudanese, the same cannot be said of team sports such as basketball and football. In recent years such sports have been a major conduit for others to hear of our country and many of our athletes have become celebrities at home. Ramciel is committed to helping spread that rightful pride in our athletes. That's why we try to publish so many photos of athletes and others who deserve attention and praise.

There is something else that should be bringing us together as a nation: floods. Water is an integral part of our nation's existence. The word Sudan comes from the Arabic sudd, which means swamp or marsh. Our marshland is important and the tribes who live in those marshes bring important qualities to our national character. However, flooding is destructive and water can be dangerous. As a nation, we need to discuss how to handle the water of our country. This subject is especially important when we recognize that climate change models suggest that South Sudan will become wetter in coming years. With the question, "Will water be our resource or our destroyer?" in mind, I am particularly pleased that this issue of Ramciel includes an interview with hydrologist Dr. Tag Elhazine.

Those of us who are part of the South Sudanese community—be we in Juba, in the hinterlands, or in the Diaspora—need to focus on our motherland as a whole. We must not allow the old thinking of London, or even that of Washington, tell us how to be a country. Instead, we must find our common cause, our shared pride, and our unique way forward. As the publisher of this magazine, I am devoted to that cause and to the future of our nation.

~*Deng Mayik Atem*
Ramciel Magazine Publisher

Available now through Africa World Books

PEACE

Peace is good leadership.
Peace is when a leader is not self-centered
and goes beyond himself for the well-being of others,
acting as servant
and not the greedy boss.

Providing services defines a peaceful society.
With good leadership, peace can conquer the odds of life.
Peace is love.
Peace is when you look at everyone just like you,
you treat everyone with love as you wish to be treated,
bringing you into harmony with others.

Peace is being humble in character.
Peace is not looking down on others,
for you do not know what tomorrow will bring.

Peace is being optimistic
and appreciative of the success of others.
With love in our hearts,
tribes, riches, and hates make no sense
in a peaceful community.

LET'S BE PEACEFUL

By Adut Bior
A senior student of Mass Communication
at Makerer University, Kapala

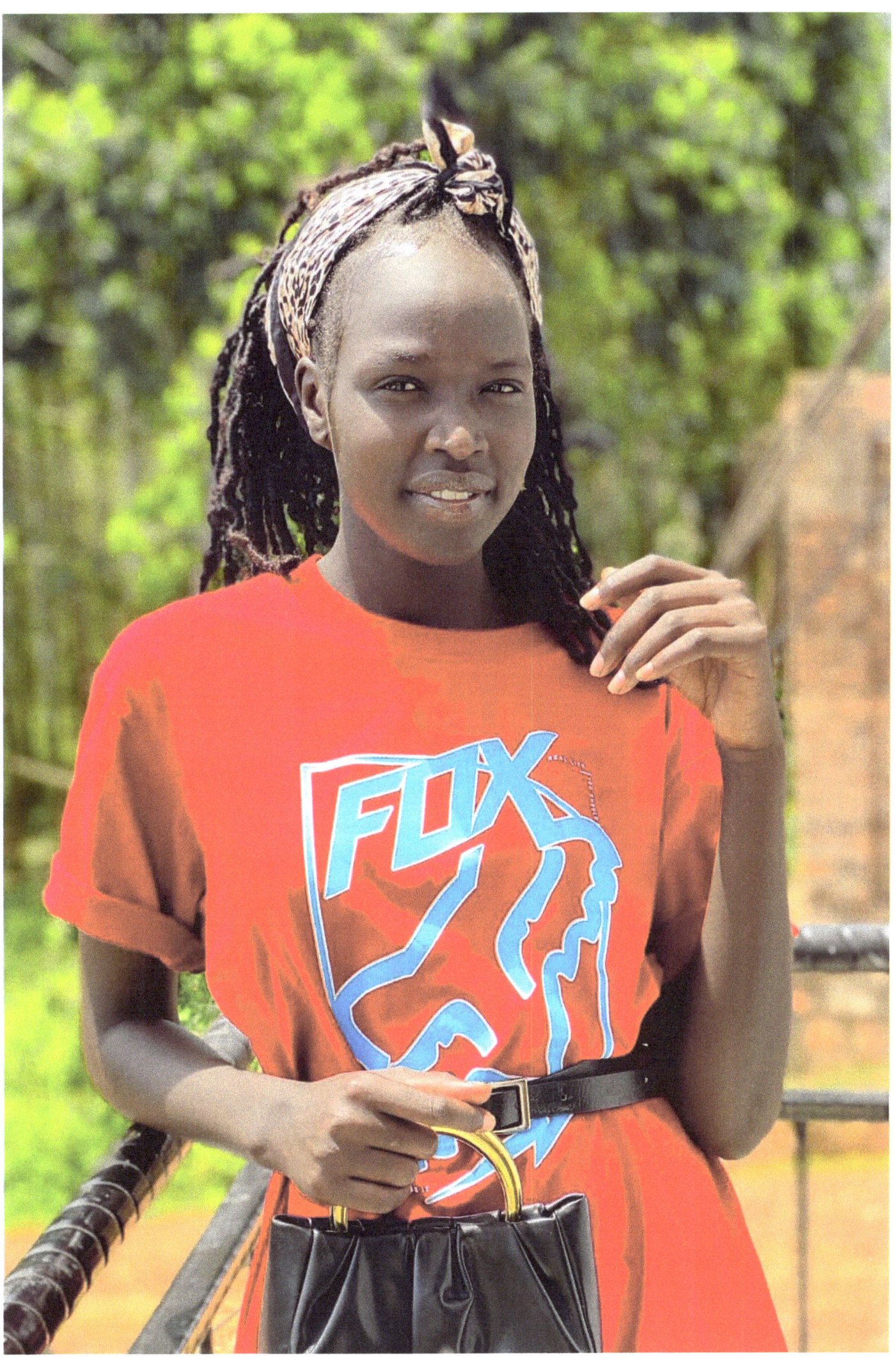

Creating an Economic Environment in South Sudan That Will Work

By Deng Mayik Atem

We propose a new goal - the creation of an economic environment that will work for our country. Currently, nothing holds our country together. The result is internecine warfare, suffering, and displacement. We need an economic system that will bring people together, and that will make each section of South Sudan aware and appreciative of the others.

Sadly, the elites of South Sudan are not interested in the nation as a whole. They are primarily interested in their families, their own communities, and their supporters. Some only care that money is in their bank accounts. They do not see themselves as South Sudanese. The South Sudanese Diaspora are Americans, Australians, Canadians, Britons, and Norwegians, but we identify more with our homeland than some of the politicians in South Sudan. For that reason, while the flow of their money is to other nations, we keep sending funds back home.

South Sudan is a nation that didn't naturally exist in the first place and no one has devoted themselves to establishing a viable state or a sense of nationhood. Part of the problem begins with tribalism and regionalism, but the problem is made much worse by money, particularly oil money. It is simply too easy for politicians to take that oil money for themselves because the amount is so tempting. With so much wealth at stake, competition to get their hands on it has been more important to many leaders than creating a viable and robust state. The objective among politicians often seems to be the last person standing is the winner of the tontine.

Adversity and trade bring people together, but sadly wealth separates them. In the absence of wealth, people can be motivated to work together to make life possible. In the village of the hungry, everyone helps to till the field. In the village of the wealthy, there is competition to see who can have the most. For South Sudan to be a better country there is a need to create an economic environment that will work and which will bring people together. The way to do that is to build common interests through trade among our communities and cooperative effort in creating trade with other countries.

To establish trade within our country, we need infrastructure: roads, bridges, railroads, trucks. We also need the means of production to be distributed to various communities. This same infrastructure is necessary to create trade with other countries. And, we need human infrastructure which comes through education and training in new methods, be they how to build a road, how to operate a machine, or how to grow a new crop. To have such training requires not only willingness among people, but also the security that allows them to take time to learn. People who are studying must be fed. Everyone must have adequate housing. And, making sure that people are healthy is necessary if they are being asked to learn and to work.

Building that infrastructure—material and human—requires two things. Capital and leadership. The capital is there in the form or resources. Not only do we have oil, but in South Sudan we have an overabundance of a resource that is becoming more and more crucial: water. We should be using water wisely to bring investment into our agricultural sector, and to sell our excess water to the countries downstream, especially Egypt which is desperate to have a secure water supply.

The problem with leadership is great. All of our tribes are gerontocracies. Our central government is centered around older leaders. Such organization is optimal when a society wants stability—although because of tribal rivalries our nation is anything but stable. However, while such an emphasis on tradition and age has served our tribes in the past, it is not working well today. Today we need change and adaptation. While we have many younger people living in the Diaspora getting modern educations, their skills and knowledge are not being utilized. In fact, when questioned about change, the current leaders tend to emphasize the need for tribal communities to maintain their old ways, even when those ways do not support more than subsistence living.

A major problem, both in developing resources and introducing new leadership, is the ongoing tension between tribes and regions. Some of those tensions go back for centuries; the rivalry between Nuer and Dinka is considered one of the most enduring inter-tribal animosities in the world. In addition to historic and cultural enmities, there is the reality of inequality. Resources, especially oil, are not distributed in an equitable manner. In order to have true economic development, investment has to be based on the best growth plan and not on where a resource might be most concentrated.

In addition to the geographical issues, there is the sense in the larger tribes that they should somehow predominate. If South Sudan had one dominant tribe, then perhaps sharing resources throughout the country might be easier. However, in our country we have not only the two lar-

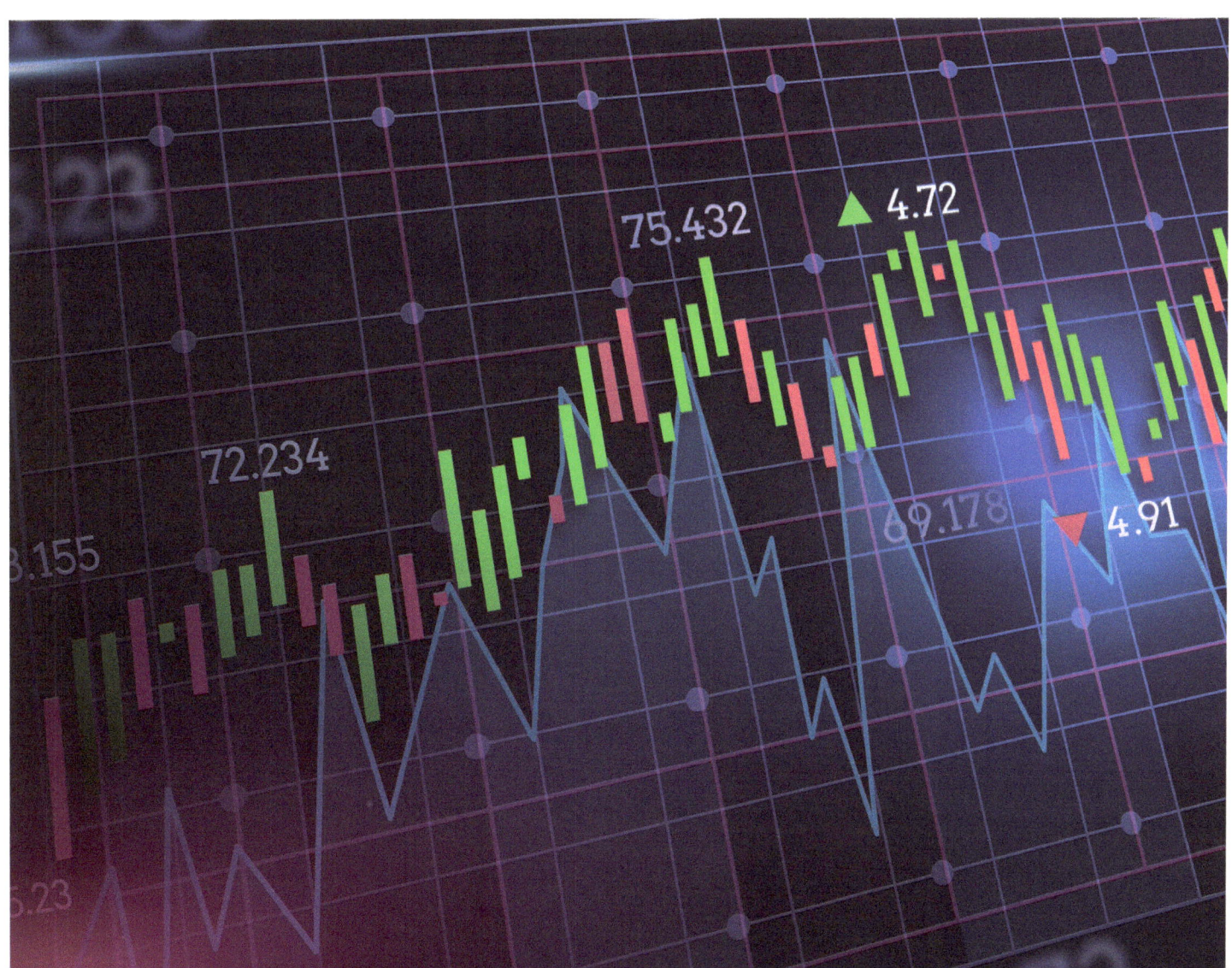

gest tribes, Dinka and Nuer, but many others. No tribe has a clear majority, or even a clear plurality. Therefore, building a sense of common cause is all the more essential.

To combat tribalism and regionalism, we need to develop a unifying educational system. We need to encourage national schools of excellence which members of all tribes attend and in which sharing of cultural differences is positive. We must also place a priority on teaching all our people a national history based on unity and a sense that we have come together as a nation. Despite the competitions and rivalries that exist, we need a national mythology that stresses our commonality.

In addition to being age-oriented, the leadership of our tribes and our government is male-dominated. Yet, often women carry the greatest burdens. While men claim the rewards, especially the right to own cows, weapons, and other tokens of status, women are carrying an enormous load. Not only should women be encouraged to take part in education and leadership, but in many communities the best way forward economically is through women-led cooperatives. Women are more likely than men to share responsibility and decision making without rivalry, and to keep the profits earned by a cooperative in the community.

The creation of cooperative businesses may seem ideologically driven, but, in fact, the evolution from such cooperative ventures into a more capitalist system is the real goal. Just as the kibbutzim of Israel were a way station in creating an incredibly strong capitalist economy, the use of a system of local community-based, women-operated cooperatives seems to be the best way forward for much of tribal sub-Saharan Africa. Indeed, some such cooperatives are already functioning successfully in other nations.

To follow this broad blueprint will require a commitment from Juba to explore new ideas, to work towards a sense of South Sudan being the expression of our mutual desire to change and grow, economically and culturally, until our nation can be a leader on our continent and in the world. Other countries such as Bangladesh and Vietnam have done so in Asia; our nation is capable of as much and more.

Athieida Media Group is a South Sudanese company incorporated in 2021. Our expertise extends beyond simple advertising from social media, branding/printing, general supply, web design and we create everything needed to build incredible results. Our experts deliver

— *Redefining your brand* —

Our Services

- Marketing research
- Radio Advertising
- Print Advertising
- Television Advertising
- Strategic Partnership
- Guerilla Marketing
- Behavioral change marketing
- Printed Collateral Branded Items (shirts, pens, etc)
- Brand Activations
- Experiential marketing.
- Content Creation & Marketing
- Social & Mobile Advertising

MOST RELIABLE ADVERTISING AGENCY

Innovative, Creative, Efficient
Value-Driven Solution

+211 917 720 042
+211 929 311 115

info@athieida.com
www.athieida.com

City Mall Malakia
3rd Floor Room 316

Rethinking Wealth as South Sudan Develops

By Deng Mayik Atem

As a young Dinka boy, I was expected to take care of my father's cows. He was not wealthy, but he did have a small herd, including one bull who had little use for me. Of course, I wasn't the only boy taking care of cows. All the men in our village prided themselves on the number and appearance of their cows.

That obsession with cows was not just among Dinka. The Nuer, Mundari, and many other tribes, both in South Sudan and elsewhere in Africa, consider cows the truest form of wealth and status. If rearing and caring for cows is traditionally important, stealing them is also part of the fabric of South Sudanese life. Not only do tribes steal cows from one another, but, worse, the Arab raiders who ravished our part of South Sudan killed our people, took all our food, and even took some people as slaves. Sadly, sometimes cattle theft involves members of the same tribe stealing from one another. Why do people steal cattle? While sometimes the cattle are stolen for food, mostly they are stolen because they represent wealth.

How much wealth can be seen in the requests that those of us living in the Diaspora receive from our families back in South Sudan. Over and over, we are asked to send money to buy cows. Now, those cows are not needed for milk; there is more milk in every village than anyone will drink. Certainly, they are seldom used for meat, at least not until they have died. Cows are only slaughtered for special rituals. Those cows represent wealth the same way that in other cultures people collect precious stones or beautiful carpets. In the modern western world, that same desire for "status wealth" leads to the purchase of art, fancy automobiles, and Rolex watches.

"Status wealth" is the way people have of saying "Hey, look at me! I'm important. I'm bigger than you." That isn't a bad thing when there is more than enough to go around. However, when other people are starving and living in want, the collection of "status wealth" can feel like an abomination. During my childhood, I spent some time at the refugee camps in Ethiopia. Life was difficult and there was often not enough to eat. The young boys were expected to work just as they did for their fathers. One of our jobs was to help build corrals for cows owned by SPLA leaders. Hungry as we may have been, as many underfed soldiers as there might have been, the leaders held on to those cows.

Not only does the keeping and hording of "status wealth" lead to envy and crime, it also means that wealth is not directed to better purposes such as clothing, feeding, and housing those in need. Another even more important function of wealth is the creation of productive means such as infrastructure, equipment, inventory, and education. I call the accumulation of such productive wealth "functional wealth." Functional wealth can belong to one person, to a company, or to a society; no matter where the ownership lies, the measure of functional wealth should be how much wealth it in turn adds. If one invests in a business, buys inventory, and then makes a profit selling that inventory, then one is adding wealth. In that case, it may seem that the only one benefitting is the businessperson, but we know that isn't true. Their customers benefit. Their suppliers also benefit. And, to the degree that they spend money on their own lives, other business owners may benefit. Of course, if they pay taxes, then the community as a whole benefits.

Going forward, the people of South Sudan face a daunting task of creating and distributing wealth. We no longer want to live in isolated villages that try to be self-sufficient but offer limited life choices. We want and need education, decent housing, clothing, healthcare, and healthy food choices. We want to be in touch with one another and with the world. That means that we need money, which is simply a way of keeping track of wealth. Storing our wealth in cows, in "status wealth" will not allow us to move forward. We need to replace the "status wealth" of cows with "functional wealth" that will allow us all to have better lives.

At the same time, we do not want to give up our identities and values. We want to continue having a sense of community and tribal identity. We certainly don't want to have all our cows disappear into slaughter houses. Our approach is to find ways to move forward while keeping touch with the past. If we work together to enrich our nation and all our people, we can still honor our traditions.

To move forward, we need the central government in Juba to help support and build infrastructure and education. Locally, we need communities to develop community-based, shared industries that can sell products to the rest of the world, but also help develop skills and quality of life for the local people. We need entrepreneurs who are able to grow small businesses that serve communities. However, central to this change is "functional wealth."

Putting together investments, especially in those local productive businesses, will not be easy. With the central government's assistance, South Sudan can attract investments from businesses in other countries and from South Sudanese living in the Diaspora. Hopefully, as the Diaspora community leads the way, the people back home will be more willing to move their wealth away from cattle and into more functional options.

There is one last caveat that must be addressed. Nobody will be willing to invest their wealth in areas that are unsafe. A central role of the national government is to provide security from crime and from natural disasters. Whether it is stopping strife between tribes or dealing with floods, we need Juba to make our nation a safe place for people to live and businesses to grow.

CONNECTING THE WORLD WITH AFRICAN LITERATURE

Africa World Books strives to spread African literature around Australia and the world. We connect authors and readers with our publishing and editing services. Everybody deserves books, which is why we continue to make them more accessible to families and individuals in our own community and around the world.

But we don't only publish African stories, **we also help with marketing, design, and selling**. Your book is important to us, so we help you get it in front of readers. We can print your book locally and with an office in South Sudan and an agent in Kenya, it is no trouble to get widespread recognition for you tale with effortless shipping throughout Africa. Plus, we also promote international writers with shows and events where they can launch their books and discuss culture, themes, and more.

WE ARE OPEN MONDAY– FRIDAY 9 AM TO 5 PM

Have a story you want to tell? We can help!

Let Us Know at:
www.africaworldbooks.com/contact-us/

Shop African Books Today at:
www.africaworldbooks.com/bookstore-home/

HAVE A SUGGESTION, QUESTION, OR CONCERN? LET US KNOW!

Unit 3, 57 Frobisher St, Osborne Park, WA 6017
☎ 0422611978
✉ info@africaworldbooks.com

EMBRACE YOUR AFRICAN HERITAGE

Africa World Books Community Education (AWBCE) unites South Sudanese and African populations of Australia to strengthen culture and keep our heritage alive for generations to come.

TITLE AND SUMMARY OF MY UPCOMING BOOK

The DIASPORA STUDENT and YOUTH FRONT

A cause that matters in your curriculum, career, and connection

The author is motivated by the desire to have diaspora youth grow up with the influence and attachment to African values and customs, and thus the contributions they can make to the African continent. This equally applies for any diaspora group. To do this, the author directly exploits and explores those academic and non-academic programs that diaspora high school and college students can participate in while abroad, either in their country of origin or any country of their choosing. The academic programs include foreign exchange, study abroad, internship and research. While participating in these academic programs, students may have opportunities to volunteer in schools, hospitals, orphanages, among others. Alternatively, the students can choose a pure non-academic program for volunteering missions abroad. On the other hand, for students who do not wish to travel but are willing to help support a cause in their country of origin or in a developing country, this book provides them with other options.

Participation in oversea programs provide students with the opportunity to improve their language skills, immerse in cultural experience, explore a country, connect with relatives, and volunteer for a disadvantaged community. The end benefits can be improved chances of college admission, job application, and career perspective.

Thank you,
David Mayom

SUPPORTING OUR COMMUNITY BY:

- Invigorating cultural values with study groups, storytelling sessions, and other events
- Connecting traditional heritage with modern services like mental health, financial literacy, and health and wellness classes
- Publishing and promoting South Sudanese and African writers as African World Books
- Encouraging Australian youth to adopt their ancestral culture and supporting parents with helpful sessions
- Preserving the Dinka language with classes and teacher training
- Hosting a reading and writing club so that we can all share our personal journeys and tales
- Inviting young people and others in our community to learn public speaking and improve their communication skills
- And More!

JOIN OUR MISSION

A community is necessary for our vision, and we need your support.

You can help by donating to our cause or simply by joining a class, attending an event, or following us on social media!

Donate Today - www.awbce.com.au/support-us
Via Bank Transfer - Africa World Books Community Education Inc.
BSB 066140, ACC 10452429

Check Out Our Facebook Page - www.facebook.com/awbce/

View Upcoming Events - www.awbce.com.au/event

Water and the Future of South Sudan

A conversation with Dr. Tag Elkhazin, an internationally recognized expert on the Horn of Africa and a senior fellow at the Norman Paterson School of International Affairs at Carleton University in Ottawa, Canada. April 24, 2022

Dr. Tag Elkhazin was born in Omdurman, Sudan. Having graduated from the University of Khartoum in 1964, he went on to study at the University of Washington, Seattle, then in Sweden and Germany. He lived for many years in London and for the last twenty-three in Canada, where, having retired, he continues to provide his services as an adjunct professor at Carleton University.

Dr. Elkhazin has been a consultant to The World Bank and to the Canadian government, and he has worked in many countries including Sudan, Saudi Arabia, Ethiopia, Kenya, Eritrea, Nigeria, and Chad. It is his goal to give back as much as he has been given by the world.

Ramciel Magazine (RM): One of the things we learned in recent interviews with others, including Deng Majok Chol who is currently a Ph.D. student at Oxford University in hydrology, is the existence of a prevailing prediction among students of climate change that there is going be more rain in South Sudan and more water. While some parts of the world are drying, others, such as our homeland, are getting wetter. This past year the flooding was horrific, many people died and many more were displaced. Can you see a scenario where this rainfall increase will benefit South Sudan?

Dr. Elkhazin (DE): It all depends on where the rain falls, and on how South Sudan deals with it. There were massive floods in South Africa; South Africa did not drain water from the main rivers. There were huge floods in British Columbia and the western part of Canada; people died and there was over 2.5 billion dollars in losses. Again, in British Columbia, we did not drain running rivers. There are cycles in the weather beyond the control of human beings, but we can mitigate the effects. There are tools we can use.

To answer your question, whatever people say is a prediction; you never know what Nature brings at the time, the day, the minutes, and the second. Nature has power that we cannot go against. So, we need to be ready to deal with the unexpected, we need to have considerable resilience and storage capability to deal with floods as they come.

RM: Are you saying that if South Sudan creates a storage system for water when there is access to drain it off, then in dry times we can utilize the stored water?

DE: That's correct. Water is a blessing. Water is one of the sources of life; both humans and animals need water to use in their bodies. There are engineering ways of dealing with water. If there is excess water, let it pass to somebody else to make use of it; that is fine. Retaining water can be pretty expensive, however, using artificial lakes and diverting tributary rivers to go to areas where the climate is drier: those are the main ways of dealing with excess rain.

Building dams is another method. There are only a few hydroelectric dams or regulating dams in South Sudan. Creating such dams would be impossibly expensive, as much as $100 billion (US). However, in cooperation with Ethiopia, a dam could possibly be built on the Baro River that could provide a water source for the Jonglei Plain. If South Sudan is to become an agricultural exporter, we will need reliable water.

RM: Is there no place in South Sudan itself where you can build such a dam?

DE: No, not one that big. There are two available places for possible dams. One is near Nimule where the Germans did a feasibility study. There is also a small rapid just north of Juba. In those two locations the river beds are rocky, so dams could be built, and water could be stored for irrigation or electric generation.

RM: Would you propose both dams be built?

DE: In theory. I hope that the meeting with government officials in Juba will be action oriented and we can discuss things that could be done.

Now, there is no money available South Sudan, and there is something called donors' fatigue. Someone from the Carter Center corrected me. He said, "It is no longer just donors' fatigue, it is also compassion fatigue, especially, when problems and political issues have continued for a long time." Then something like Ukraine comes along and South Sudan becomes a second level priority. The last grant from the World Bank signed in March 2022 was for $120 million over five years. If you want to build dams, 25-30 million dollars yearly will only go so far.

RM: What are the possibilities of getting Cairo to help? Egypt is most in need of our water and has

support from the U.S. They desperately need a lot of water, primarily because of what has been happening in Ethiopia. Could Juba and Cairo form a partnership?

DE: You are right, this is the elephant in the room. It takes us to the concept of the Jonglei Canal. The canal was envisioned in 1904 by British engineers, and it was a colonial concept. But we can change the functionalities and probably the design. If you want to build a villa, you don't get a map and a chat wheel for a store or for a tukul. You need to design a structure for the purpose that you want. So, the design in the eighties used machines and dug about two-thirds of the canal. The sole purpose was to drain between four and ten cubic meters of water into the Nile to go to Egypt. At that time there was no consideration of partnership or collaboration.

If South Sudan were to dig such a canal, first, we would need to decide the rules of the game. There is a power imbalance in the region when you consider the gross domestic product, military power, and political clout. Egypt is not a joke.

Consider Israel as a model. There are eight million Israelis that, since 1948, have been standing in the face of two hundred twenty million Arabs. In the same way, South Sudan needs to know our rights and ask, "Why should we let the water go?" This could bring us to the Nile Basin Initiative.

RM: What is the Nile Basin Initiative?

DE: The Nile Basin Initiative is a coordinated effort by ten countries: Burundi, DR Congo, Egypt, Ethiopia, Kenya, Rwanda, South Sudan, Sudan, Tanzania, and Uganda. Eritrea participates as an observer. The Nile Basin Initiative's main focus is the rights and benefits of this great waterway. What are the rights of the source countries, and what are the benefits for those who need the water? The goal has to be equity.

Building a hotel, hospital, or tiny power generation station that produces 100 kHz is peanuts. You are trading a fresh water table with a constant flow of water. Egypt needs to be fair and honest with South Sudan if they want part of the benefits of the water rights of South Sudan. They have got to give equitable benefits to South Sudan and not the tiny things the Middle East does. There really is no comparison. What's at stake is technical capacity. Egypt is one of the world's masters in water politics and policy.

Water sciences are divided into hydrology and hydraulics. Hydrology is the discharge of the quantity of water, and it's a separate, soft science. Hydraulics is the energy in the water and the production of hydroelectric power. Egypt is the master of both, so there is a power imbalance and a military imbalance between our countries, but, more importantly, a knowledge imbalance.

There is a growing awareness in Juba because the President has asked me to visit Juba to make a presentation on my general knowledge and understanding of water issues. The contract for that presentation is under negotiation with Dr. Barnabas Marial.

Historically, there are two international agreements that we need to know about. One entered into in 2017-2018 deals with transborder rivers and navigation. An earlier one, from 1959, acts as if the only two countries that matter are Egypt

and Sudan. It is as if South Sudan, which didn't exist at that time, Ethiopia where 86 percent of the Nile begins its flow, and the other countries of the Initiative don't matter. It is clearly the result of colonialist thinking.

Going forward, we need to have agreements with our neighbors about the rivers and the use of our water. Those agreements have to meet the needs of South Sudan not just the countries down river from us. If we are to go forward with a canal to help Egypt, we have to make sure there is a fair return for us.

RM: Clearly there has to be an agreement, and it can't be an agreement that was created before South Sudan existed. It would have to work with Ethiopia as well. Addis Ababa's participation is crucial. However, Juba is a key player. Do you think the politicians in Juba are aware of the issues? Are they interested in coming up with real solutions, or are they just looking for what they can get? The four star hotel currently being built in Juba by Egyptians seems to be a distraction from the real goals of development.

DE: I believe we have no option but to work with the government of the day. The current government in Juba is what we have. They have the military power and there is significant tribal support for the incumbent government. We have no options but to work with them.

The collective knowledge and information about water in South Sudan is limited. In 2008, I made a presentation on the Nile River water, and Michael Makuei, then minister of legal affairs, attended the event. I told him that there were a lot of agreements about the Nile and its water. He said, "Tag, we do not know what you are talking about because we do not have copies of the arrangements." That includes the White Nile, part of which generates from South Sudan. There is a gap even in the availability of documentation, to say nothing of the gap in knowledge. We need a coordinated, multiple-disciplined approach.

The subject of water is not just about the Jonglei Canal. Floods, water for irrigation, transportation, power generation: all these are connected and must be integrated. We need to plan for that, and the development capacity is not yet there. South Sudan needs help with our water, technically and politically. We need to differentiate water politics and water policy, and a more capable, targeted approach to dealing with neighboring countries.

Egyptians are concerned over Sudan's share of the Nile. Since the 1959 agreement, Sudan was to have 18.9 billion cubic meters. Sudan never used more than 12 billion cubic meters of water. But, since 1964, between 6 to 6.5 billion cubic meters of water from Sudan's share was going downriver to Egypt. That same agreement talks about 18.5 billion cubic meters going to Sudan and what is now South Sudan. Is there a share in that for South Sudan? No one ever asks that question, let alone gets an answer.

Meanwhile, the Egyptians are panicking because of the Grand Ethiopian Renaissance Dam and the massive lakes behind it. If Sudan and Ethiopia can develop water storage and keep part of the water behind the GERD, Egypt will be short six billion cubic meters of water. Egyptians know that, so Cairo has started massive desalinization projects, which are costly. How will Egypt respond to that dam? Will there be a military response?

Clearly, water, and specifically the water of the Nile, is an important political issue.

RM: You said there needs to be more awareness of political focus in South Sudan on addressing these issues of water policy and water politics. Is there a possibility that external forces from Cairo or elsewhere might come into play if the South Sudanese government develops a water plan? Could this lead to outside forces trying to overthrow the government?

DE: That is always a possibility since outsiders are often at work in countries like ours. For example, while the GERD was an Ethiopian vision in 1936, before the Second World War the President of the

United States proposed funding the dam. That is history now, but it shows how other governments can potentially get involved.

If the government of South Sudan is overthrown, the problems won't go away because the issue of water and how to allocate it would remain. Could South Sudan become like some of the Latin American countries whose governments have been routinely interfered with and overthrown, especially by America? That is possible, and it is one reason we need to create awareness of our nation as a country among the people. The people are constant, and governments are transitional, so our target is to create a broad base of information and knowledge about the value of water. Of course, South Sudan has many problems, many divisions, and internal animosities. Those problems are more likely to tear our country apart than is foreign intervention.

RM: Since there is the possibility of foreign intervention because water is so valuable to Egypt, and Egypt is so helpful to Western powers, the European Union, Great Britain, Canada, and the United States, do we just sacrifice South Sudan and would that be terrible?

DE: At one of the Nile Basin meetings in Addis Ababa, Hossein Mubarak who was then President of Egypt came to the meeting with a general who was the minister of defense. Some people laughed. President Mubarak said, "No, this is what it means to us and for us. The Nile water is national security, and this is the top man in the army, so he is part of our team."

I take your point seriously. The population of Egypt is a 105 million, the third most populated country in Africa after Nigeria and Ethiopia. Egypt's economy is under pressure as reflected by current president El-Sisi's taking control over some of the agencies that hamper businesses. Things need a little bit of time to settle down, but the last thing he would want is people crying for water because there is no water for irrigation.

As to the likelihood of military intervention, they would have to go through another country—Sudan, Chad, Central Africa Republic—in order enter South Sudan, and the people of South Sudan would put up a fight. Look at Ukraine and Russia; Russia is that big and Ukraine is that small, but the Ukrainians have put up a fight to defend their land. It will be difficult if such a thing occurs, and that is why people from all sides better be thinking of an amicable solution such as professional mediation. However, no one should be taken for a ride, especially not the South Sudanese.

South Sudan has two assets. One is oil which is non-renewable; the barrel that you take, it is gone forever. Abyei has almost no oil left; their wells are drying out. As you go south, the ground there still has some oil but, as it is removed, the area is so wet that water will get into the oil wells. It will be very expensive to get this oil.

The second asset is renewable and it is water. As long as there are good rains, more water will come to South Sudan. If you look at a map of South Sudan, western Equatoria is called the green belt. It is the green belt for one reason - there is a lot of rainfall. That rainfall lends itself to good agriculture, to good crop growth.

The first step for the government of South Sudan should be to become informed of the resources we have and how to manage those resources.

RM: When you speak of resources and managing them properly, can you suggest some of your concerns about managing water as a resource?

DE: Proper water policy is essential. A policy document, issued in 2007 and revised by Isaac Liawell in 2011, discusses where the water would go, who would get what. There was no grand policy consideration, no consideration of how to deal with this water. For example, there is shallow, underground water and there is deep-bore water. One step we need to take is to analyze what lies under the great pools of water, what lies under the sudd. In many places, there is no good rock forma-

tion to form barriers around underground water so shallow water is not a resource of potable water for communities. In many instances, wells have been dug for villages that were not deep enough. Soon after the wells were dug they went dry, and the good people of those communities were scammed.

An important part of such a survey will be to identify underground structures that allow us to create good reservoirs so we have better control over water, and have it available to move to where it is needed, be it for agriculture, drinking, or even to provide to our neighbors.

We also need to think about how to protect our water from pollution. That especially includes protecting our water from the pollution that comes from drilling for oil.

And, of course, we must have a clear policy regarding our neighbors and how the water is to be shared, a policy that will be fair to our country and to others. So, when South Sudan's government starts dealing with water issues there must be knowledge, information, research, and planning.

RM: One of the things we have learned is that a lot of the money from selling South Sudan's oil is going towards buying more weapons when it should be used to purchase education, develop water management techniques, build dams or develop other resources. Instead, it is being wasted on the least useful of all items, guns.

DE: That's correct. When the 2005 agreement was signed, South Africa offered to train bush generals, the resistance, and the freedom fighter's leaders. The goal was to transform military people into civilians who can deal with civilian lives. Not many people were willing to take the course. However, one of the people who went was the late Dr. Justin Yac Arop, who was a medical doctor. Sadly, many people claimed they knew it all, that they didn't need South Africans or that course. I think it was a fatal mistake that led to a military mentality, the belief that the gun can deal with everything. It is well-known internationally that the soldiers in South Sudan are among the most trigger-happy in the world. If anything upsets them, they start shooting. I was talking to a group of young people in Mading Bor. They all want to be soldiers. Everybody feels he has power if he has a gun but not if he has a university degree.

Canada has the most university graduates per capita globally; second is Israel. Israel has eight million people, a small piece of land, and tension all the time. Still, they have high per capita income. There is hardly any scientific interest you won't find in Israel. Yes, the country has a strong army, but it has been education that has truly sustained Israel.

Our resources are decreasing, and we must invest in education. Consider Japan - after Japan surrendered in 1945, the emperor called the wise people and said, "Our country is destroyed; what can we do?" The answer to his question was to give what money and resources they had to teachers and education. Japan began its rebirth by backward engineering, using its students to study how other countries made things. At first, the world thought that Japanese products were rubbish, but now it is a powerful economy, one of the greatest in the world.

In South Sudan, both before and since independence, millions and millions of dollars in aid and revenue from oil sales have been wasted; some through dishonesty and some through mismanagement. Today, our oil production is down, under 120,000 barrels per day. Clearly, we need to do better, not just in oil production but in using the revenue from it. We need to be investing in quality education. Take the example of the University of Juba, try to find it in the international ranking of universities. It is non-existent. We need to attract the best teachers for our universities, the best from the Diaspora, and the best from other countries.

RM: How might highly educated South Sudanese contribute to their nation's development? Are young people being discouraged from becoming politically involved?

DE: Social awareness is complex, especially in a developing country like South Sudan. General Olusegun Obasanjo of Nigeria was president twice. He was president after the revolution after he served as an army general. He left the presidency as an honorable man and then became President again, this time by election. I met him in Addis

Ababa, and I invited him for lunch. Obasanjo is a giant; he is probably 6'6 or 6'7. If you see him, you better step aside. As we were having lunch, I was talking about African leaders. Every time I said, "African leaders," Obasanjo looked at me with a start. I asked if I was saying something wrong saying "African leaders". He looked at me and said, "Look here, young man, in Africa there are no leaders; there are only rulers."

Sadly, those were words of wisdom. Leaders listen to the people. Leaders have modesty. Leaders always have the best interests of their citizens at heart. Do we have leaders in South Sudan? We have good people, and now we need to take these good and creative people to make a national leadership.

We need government to show good leadership. If you go outside of Juba, there is no tarmac except one road. There are no real schools, no power generation facilities, and certainly no universities. So, all 21 billion dollars was lost one way or another, and nobody is going to give South Sudan another 21 billion dollars. We need government that is accountable. Every time I see my prime minister in Canada wasting money—it is my tax money—I get angry. I write to him and complain that the money isn't being used properly. One time after I wrote to him, he didn't respond within a week, so I called him up and said, "We put you in that seat and we can take you out of it."

South Sudan needs leaders, and leaders who will listen to the people of the country.

RM: Thank you, Dr. Tag Elkhazin for spending this time with us and for your informative answers.

DE: I spent more than twenty years in what is now South Sudan. I built the White Nile Brewery in Wau, which was the first development project in that area. I loved the local beer as soon as I tasted it. Then Jaafar Nimeiry decided to go crazy and he decided that no one was allowed to drink, not in the whole country. The factory was a hundred percent complete, and we even did the tests. Sadly, now it is like it never existed.

I built many rainwater harvest structures and wells for the pastoralists, probably 120 to 130 wells in my career. I lived under the trees and never travelled with security. I always travelled in my own car and was never abused or insulted. The people of South Sudan are very good and deserve the best on earth. For me, helping the people of South Sudan is not about money. I don't need money, thank God. So, anytime I can be helpful, I am available. Thank you so much for having me.

A Conversation with Paramount Chief dr. Abuk Deng Mashama Angui

South Sudanese-American, Residing in Buffalo, NY, USA
(Nursing Degree and Ph.D. in Public Administration)
Interview by Sultana Abuk Deng Macham Angui,
July 18, 2022.

Ramciel Magazine (RM): Your father was the first person to hold this role as the Paramount Chief of the sixty-four tribes.

PCA: Yes. Correct.

RM: You are a woman and a Dinka. How typical is that for somebody in a leadership role among South Sudanese?

PCA: It is not just being a Dinka leader, but it is about the whole of the sixty-four tribes of South Sudan that I represent.

RM: So you represent all the sixty-four tribes?

PCA: Correct. This position is quite different. Traditionally, only men are usually crowned as the traditional chiefs of their respective communities, but the world has changed. The modern world has another way of looking at things, and that's how I ended up being a paramount chief representing all of our ten states and three administrative areas. I am a South Sudanese—American, and I see myself playing the greatest role back home in the motherland, especially with the skills, knowledge, and experiences I have learned here in my adopted country and to take them back to help my people. South Sudan needs all of us; therefore, it is crucial to incorporate modernization and traditional values to forge a better understanding of our time.

RM: So, you are, in a real sense, a major political player in South Sudan, except you are doing it in a traditional role rather than an elected parliamentary role?

PCA: Yes, basically, I am attached to the government; whatever the government needs from other chief councils and me, we are always there to support the government. We help in many ways because those sixty-four tribes reside in ten states and three administrative areas of South Sudan. Each tribal community has its norms and values that define who they are. Therefore, we, the traditional representatives, always want to play a positive role by encouraging and fostering a good working relationship between the government and traditionalists. Our job is to support the government and the communities, and help in situations like land disputes, marriages, and even murders.

RM: You mentioned land disputes, which are sometimes very contentious in South Sudan and especially in Juba, where the locals believe that their lands are being taken by their fellow countrymen and women from different areas. We thought lands are supposed to belong to the communities.

PCA: Correct, you are absolutely right the land belongs to the community and it is an important matter that require the national government to do its best by making sure that citizens' rights are respected.

"WE ARE ALWAYS THERE TO SUPPORT THE GOVERNMENT"

RM: What do you see as the role of those in the Diaspora?

PCA: Currently, I am working with all sixty-four tribes in the Diaspora; I am trying my best to connect with our people in Australia, Canada, Europe, the United States, and other areas where South Sudanese may be. We try to encourage our people in the Diaspora because our people are faced with challenges because of the cultural interaction and political makeup of most of our hosting countries.

RM: You have a great deal of authority.

PCA: Thank you.

RM: Other communities have their traditional customary laws, such as that of Dinka's wathalal that govern Dinka traditional marriage, among other norms and values. This is just an example. How does such a rule apply if each tribe has such rules in their respective communities?

PCA: Well, gunoon wathalal applies to only Dinka communities. As for the other tribes, we work with whatever they have as their customary laws. We don't have any universal or traditional customary laws for all tribes except the National Constitution of the Republic of South Sudan.

RM: What do you do when a member of a cattle herding community elopes with a member of a non-cattle herding community? How are the marriage values determined? Do you have a way your leadership would mitigate the dispute or settlement?

PCA: In our office, we have representatives from different states, so whatever the case may be, I usually call the representative to get the best possible way of handling that matter, if it warrants punishment or needs to be settled by the courts.

RM: So, you are enforcing the laws, and the laws being enforced in the Nuer community are different than the laws enforced in the Bari, Dinka, or Shilluk communities, but you are all committed to the idea that traditional rules should be continued?

PCA: Correct.

RM: Then you have a government in Juba that makes other laws. How do you coordinate with the Juba government, like if it said we are going to change the laws?

PCA: The government always follows the local tradition.

RM: Since there are sixty-four tribes in South Sudan, how many members of chiefs' groups are there?

PCA: There are a total of thirteen representatives. I have representatives from all ten and three administrative areas of Abyei, Greater Pibor, and Ruweng Administrative Area. Those thirteen members represent the voices of tribal communities by working directly with the national government, state governments, and local governments.

RM: How often do you meet with these groups of people?

PCA: It depends, it could be one or twice a month, but sometimes we have emergency meetings on whatever the case may be.

RM: There is a vast South Sudanese community in the Diaspora. Besides yourself here in America, do you have other representatives living in the Diaspora?

PCA: We have representatives worldwide, wherever South Sudanese are. Although we don't have a budget to sustain our organization, we still hope to solicit support from communities and our hosting countries. Regardless, we are united and determined to continue coordinating our activities whenever and wherever possible.

RM: That sounds like a tremendous job.

PCA: Indeed, it is.

RM: You also have children and are married; plus you are studying for a doctorate, aren't you?

PCA: My husband and I are blessed with eight children - five girls and three boys. We arrived in the United States in 1999, and both of us went to community colleges. We transferred to universities where we obtained our bachelor's and masters' degrees. I earned my doctorate.

RM: What was your Ph.D. in?

PCA: Public Administration.

RM: That's certainly the right thing for what you are doing.

PCA: Thanks.

RM: I am curious. You are working very hard, and I hope you are getting remunerations so you can feed your eight children? Who pays your salary?

PCA: No one is paying me, but I am still working on it. I am volunteering now, and hopeful my team and I will get paid. I hope that by using this forum in Ramciel Magazine I can get my voice out there, and someone will help support us.

RM: What do you know about the Courts of Traditional Authorities leaders (COTAL) in Warrap State?

PCA: Yes, I know about it. It started during the time of my father.

RM: Did Chiefs get paid? Who paid them? Also, did Chiefs get vehicles from the central government or state governments?

PCA: Yes, I heard that they got some vehicles before, but it was one time. It wasn't all the chiefs who received cars; it was only the representatives of ten states plus the administrative areas. That was during my father's reign. But I should add, there were some issues with those vehicles. It was challenging to maintain them, so the owners sold them. As for me, I haven't received anything yet.

RM: You are now the traditional leader and you represent the traditional leadership. Are there other countries in Africa, or the rest of the world, where there are people similar to yourself and the other chiefs?

PCA: There are several African countries, Ghana and Botswana are among the few nations that exercise similar traditional leadership, but they do it in their way, and basically, they are attached to their respective governments. Mine is quite different now because I am working with the government in South Sudan and the Diaspora communities in other hosting countries.

RM: Have you had any role in your contact with any international organization or agency such as the UN or any others?

PCA: Not really, but I was told to get a 501(C)3 or charitable organization status in the US. We are currently working on obtaining the organization's position. We registered it already, but we still have several things to complete.

RM: If you could make one change in South Sudan as it is now, what would you change?

PCA: I would wish to see some change in the economy. A lot of our people are hungry. Children, women, and everyone go to bed with empty stomachs every night; almost half of the population is food insecure. I would love to see our people prosper to make a better living for themselves and their families.

RM: Given the traditional culture of the tribal people of South Sudan, do you see the tribes changing their cultures to adjust to the modern economy of the world?

PCA: Yes. Possibilities are there. However, it will take some time, slowly and gradually. I was in South Sudan for more than seven months; I saw changes leading to economic advancement.

RM: Regarding conflicts among the Dinka Communities back home: What do you think could be a solution to resolve all those conflicts, especially with the current conflict between Ngok and Twic Mayardit? Have you reached out to both communities?

PCA: I haven't talked directly to their chiefs, but I am communicating with my Juba team and both communities at different levels. I told them that this conflict should and must stop. We don't condone any violence. Ngok and Twic are one family, and they need to understand that.

RM: Do you see a way for Sub-Saharan Africa and Saharan Africa (Arab-Africa) to work together, or do you think there will always be an enmity?

PCA: They can work together on some points, but in years to come I don't know. We have experienced five decades of war with the Arabs in North Sudan. I don't think we are ready to share anything political. Business is okay, there could be some cooperation among us, but I don't see any chance of reunification with Sudan.

RM: You don't see any kind of Federation with Sudan?

PCA: No possibility of federation with Sudan, especially after five decades of war with Northern Sudan.

RM: Do you think traditional societal leaders can help solve the current political crisis in South Sudan?

PCA: Yes. They have, and they are still working on it.

RM: As the traditional chiefs, what are you doing about the land grab in Juba? The locals are complaining about their land being taken away by the members of other communities, especially by the Dinka and the Nuer. From the perspective of an overall Paramount Chief, how could that problem be solved?

PCA: It is quite a challenge. But we recognize the change from traditional to modern economies, and that one issue will be the task we see our group having a significant role in ensuring everyone is dealt with fairly.

RM: Have you ever met or discussed any of your roles with the Jieng Council of Elders?

PCA: I spoke with Dr. Ajoudit and Dr. Ajou Deng Akueny. He appreciated my leadership and congratulated me. He is my supporter. I always talk with him, especially when I am in Juba.

RM: There are individuals here in the Diaspora who inherited the chieftaincy after their fathers passed away in South Sudan, and they were crowned successors. Are you aware of those chiefs?

PCA: Yes, I have talked to some of them. Several young men inherited chieftaincy from their fathers. As I mentioned earlier, I have a chiefs' council team here in the Diaspora. So, I am working with them.

RM: Will you appoint new chiefs to represent each community in the Diaspora?

PCA: Most of the communities have their representatives, but if there is any community that doesn't have a representative, then I can work with that community and ask their leaders to select or appoint someone to represent them.

A Conversation with Achuei Deng Ajing

June 28, 2022, Washington. USA

RM: Hello, Achuei Deng Ajing. Welcome to America.

ADA: Thank You. I am glad to be here.

R.M: Who is Achuei Deng Ajing?

ADA: Achuei Deng Ajing is a South Sudanese musician residing in Juba. She is originally from Wunrok Adiang Payam, Twic Mayardit County of Warrap State, South Sudan.

R.M: Is this your first time in the United States?

ADA: Correct, this is the first I have ever visited the U.S.

R.M: What do you think of America?

ADA: I love it. It is beautiful, and the people are lovely.

R.M: How did it feel?

ADA: Well, it felt fantastic. I enjoyed every moment. I'm in love with this beautiful country.

R.M: Who's your favorite, influential artist among South Sudanese artists?

ADA: The late Teresa Nyankol Mathiang.

R.M: From whom did you inherit your talent?

ADA: My maternal grandmother. She was a great traditional singer in the Adiang-Mayom section of Twic Mayardit.

RM: Do you think South Sudanese culture maintains itself here in the USA?

ADA: I was impressed with how our South Sudanese communities in America keep up with their traditional values, especially in their efforts to teach the youngest to keep up with their cultures.

R.M: What would you like people in the USA to know about what is happening in our homeland?

ADA: Well, we are keeping it real in the Motherland, and want them to continue visiting home because there is nothing like home. So, keep up with your roots!

R.M: What would you like the people in South Sudan to know about what is happening in America?

ADA: Try to visit America when you have a chance. It is a beautiful country with friendly and wonderful people.

R.M: While you have been in the U.S., which of your songs have been the most requested?

ADA: Mading Aweil, Rumbek, Bahr El Ghazal, and Apeth Nya.

R.M: Are you planning to write a new song based on your experiences in America?

ADA: Well, I'm thinking about it. We shall see when the time is right.

R.M: How was your Las Vegas experience?

ADA: Las Vegas was fabulous. A beautiful city with tall skyscrapers like NYC.

R.M: And what did you think of NYC?

ADA: NYC was amazing. I visited there after my show in Phoenix, Arizona, in April. Then we drove through New York City again several days before I left Washington, D.C., for Juba. After my last event in Boston, Massachusetts, on June 25, my USA tour team decided that we should drive instead of flying because they wanted me to go through several states and cities on our way to Washington, D.C. I agreed, and it was a wonderful experience.

R.M: What would you tell other musicians about America?

ADA: Come to America so you can discover how much love the South Sudanese in the Diaspora have for you. The South Sudanese in America have access to many ways of listening to music. For instance, they have no issues with running out of MBS Data, they have access to electricity 24/7, and WiFi is available everywhere you go. When I was on the highway where cities are miles away, I was still connected.

R.M: Does the American work ethic inspire the South Sudanese in the struggle for our country?

ADA: Absolutely, one can tell how hard people work here in this country. Hard work always pays off, and I commend Americans for their hard work in developing their nation.

R.M: What were your favorite foods in America?

ADA: There are various foods in America. However, I love hamburgers from McDonald's, Jack in the Box, and Burger King. I also love Texas Long-Horn baby back ribs, Chinese food, and Denny's. You can tell that I have gained some weight since I came here. Eating all these delicious foods has been like running a marathon of restaurants!

R.M: Did anything particular impress you about America?

ADA: People are usually busy doing positive things for themselves, their families, and their communities. I commend them for that. I appreciate those who took time off their busy schedules and drove, or flew, to attend the events organized on my behalf. I cannot say thank you enough for their efforts.

R.M: What would you have done if you had not become a musician?

ADA: Play professional volleyball and study to become a medical doctor.

R.M: What do you feel is the best song you have ever released, and why?

ADA: Well, most of the songs I have composed come deep from the bottom of my heart. That makes them all the best.

R.M: Which musician or musicians would you like to collaborate with next?

ADA: Johnson Jok Lal, Emmanuek Kembe, and others as well

R.M: What do you think of the music industry in South Sudan?

ADA: I would like to see the artistic community grow and be recognized in the world. Our music industry could be better developed because we are a young nation. We have so many talented young people eager for opportunities to showcase their artistic skills. They should be heard.

R.M: Are there any humanitarian projects you are working on now?

ADA: Currently, we are working on a water pump, or borehole, in Rumbek National Secondary School in Lake State. It was a commitment that I promised students and staff last year during my first-ever visit to Rumbek National. The process has already started and, hopefully, it should be completed next month by the time I return to Juba.

R.M: What is your advice for South Sudanese youth?

ADA: Stay focused and be agents of change for our beloved nation. The future belongs to the young. Therefore, it is they who must embrace unity, peace, love, and harmony.

R.M: What would you most like to see change in South Sudan?

ADA: I would like to see economic development; to see everybody doing better. And, I want us to stop killing each other. We must understand that we are all one people, and we can keep our diversity while growing as a country.

R.M: Is there anything I left out that I did not ask.

ADA: No. Thank you.

R.M: Achuei Deng Ajing, thank you very much for taking the time to answer these questions. Please have a safe trip back to the Motherland.

THE PRIDE OF SOUTH SUDAN

All who identify with South Sudan can take pride in her athletes. The men's basketball team have qualified for the 2023 FIBA cup. Having bested Senegal and Egypt, and with outstanding play by Nuni Omot, who had the highest average points per game, Deng Acuoth, with highest average rebounds, and Sunday Deth, highest average assists, our South Sudanese basketballers had the most points scored of any team in the round robin and the highest percentage of free throws. And there is no question that the leadership of Luol Deng and the head coach must be credited for this great showing by the national team. These are the kind of results that can get all South Sudanese, regardless of tribe, region, or place of current abode, cheering.

As a new nation with so many tribal and ethnic groups, we need to build a common identity. We need to create a national mythos. What better place to start than with our wonderful athletes; not just our basketball players but also our footballers—with a special shoutout to the Bright Starts—and wrestlers—especially those in Australia; and let us not forget our great women athletes as well, the Bright Starlets. If there is one thing positive about the diaspora, it has been the opportunity that so many of our compatriots and women have had to take part in sports.

Wherever we live, no matter from what tribe or region we hail, let us take delight in the accomplishments of our teams and let us all encourage the youth of South Sudan to take part in sports.

~by Deng Mayik Atem

BRIGHT STAR ATRAS
KUSH AIR
THANK YOU FOR SUPPORTING OUR TEAM
WELLCOME BACK HOME BRIGHT STARS

Can Sudan Survive?

By Deng Mayik Atem
Author of 'Jumping Over the Ram'

Once again, Sudan is bathed in the blood of civil war. Once again, an apparent alliance has fallen apart in the streets of Khartoum. Only a dozen years ago, the country was torn in two when, after many years of bloodshed, the people of South Sudan overwhelmingly voted for independence. At that time many of the SPLM supporters were from the Blue Nile, Darfur and Nubia. Those people were denied the opportunity to join the new country. The political geography of the Europeans was allowed to overrule the demographic geography of Africa. Sadly, that has happened so many times in recent history.

Sub-Saharan Africa is a continent of tribes. No place is that clearer than in the Sudans, especially South Sudan. Sudan is an un-mixture of Arabs and tribal Africans. Many of those tribal Africans are Muslim. Perhaps that's why the powers that brokered South Sudanese independence did not see a need to allow more of the Black-skinned people of Sudan to break away. Certainly, another reason was the insistence from Khartoum that the two countries had to share the oil that had recently been discovered.

At any rate, the Africans of South Sudan are never going to find equality with the Arab majority. Without the army of Great Britain garrisoning the land of Kush, there will always be a tension between Arab and African. One part of that tension is Sharia. The Arab interpretation of Islam tends to be much stricter and more rigid than that of the tribal Muslims. While the Islamic population of South Sudan is a small minority, they are more welcome to practice their faith as they see fit than are the African-Muslims of the north.

Another source of the strain is quite simply the sense that people are different. When the Europeans took control of our continent, they did not set boundaries based on where tribes lived or even on uniting language groups. Their borders were primarily based on their "explorations" and what they considered natural boundaries, like rivers. To use a waterway as a border flies in the face of pre--European history when tribes routinely settled on both sides of a river and used that water as a connection rather than a separation.

What will happen—not so much in the short as the long term? It is difficult to predict. In the short run, there will no doubt be another truce, another joint government, and then another falling out. But, in the long run, Sudan can only be fully stable if there is an end of Arab domination or if the Arabs decide to really see Africans as their equals. Honestly, I do not see the latter ever happening. Nor do I see the African Sudanese of Darfur, Funj, and Nubia ever accepting submission.

Could the African communities leave Sudan and become a separate state? Would the world support them as it did South Sudan? Would that state include the northern part of what is now South Sudan? Or perhaps, could those communities join and expand South Sudan? If they did, would that make South Sudan more stable and more democratic than it is now?

These are questions that need discussion. These are paths toward the future that need exploration. Two things are clear: the mess left in Africa by the European colonizers has not yet been cleared away, and the people of the region will need to come together and reach an agreement on how to move forward.

May God save Sudan.

Kenya's Elections

By Achol Maker

Should politics in Kenya be a national outfit in terms of mentorship? Elections are a democratic right in most democratic states and Kenya over the years has proved the importance of upholding this right. Looking at History of the shady violence that took place in the 2007 polls, nations around the world have been peering into Kenya's compound_ some with the intention of devouring on its failure and a few with the hope that peace prevails. Nevertheless, Kenya proved a peaceful country in 2022 polls, an outcome that brimmed other East African countries with a mixture of admiration and green-eyes.

This year's elections saw a competitive race between Hon. Raila Amolo Odinga and Dr. William Samoei Ruto- The former deputy president and a first timer in the presidential race. Hon. Ruto, a man whose friend (Former president Uhuru Kenyatta) became a foe and Hon. Raila, a man who shook hands with his 'enemy' to maintain peace.

With Raila Odinga- the heart of Kenya's democracy vying for the fifth time in a row, many in their hearts of hearts hoped for him to finally sco-op first place and rule the glorious nation. Opposite to his expectations, William Ruto dubbed 'The Hustler' was announced president and just like the other times, Mr. Odinga took to the Supreme court to challenge the results.

Although four members of the election board denounced the results, a consensus was reached by the seven judges and Ruto's win was upheld. A verdict that many Kenyans accepted and the former prime minister half-heartedly had to be walked home.

A betrayal you may feel. 'This old man has done so much for Kenya!' You might say. But what does democracy say? The 'AYES' have it! And presidency is not promised in politics.

How has Kenya done this? How is it possible to hold peaceful elections, have opposition parties, have homes not broken into during this period, limbs broken? How is it possible for any citizen to have the privilege of downloading election documents in real-time and see them for themselves? Many African countries couldn't cease to wonder and South Sudan wasn't any different.

Over the years, Kenya has hosted thousands of South Sudanese and no matter how loose their mouths itched their opinions on Kenya's election were not allowed to leave their premises. It wasn't that Kenya didn't have the freedom of speech, but how do you sweep your neighbor's compound when your own is dirty?

South Sudan is a young country at its verge of becoming a teenager. The only election the country has seen was that of making South Sudan an independent country. Eight months to the speculated first general elections and the Revitalized Agreement on Resolution of the Conflict in the Republic of South Sudan (R-ARCSS) is extended for two more years.

Will this be worth the wait? None of us knows but Sir Abraham Lincoln says, "The ballot is stronger than the bullet." Should we give this a shot? Perhaps YES!

Akon Esther

A Profile

I am Akon Esther, a South Sudanese. I believe myself to be an openminded, honest person desiring authenticity from those I love. I was brought up in a very disciplined atmosphere surrounded by family. Most of my core values in life, which I still carry, were created then.

I have completed a Bachelor's Degree in Human Resource Management and a Nano Degree in Digital Marketing. While I was still in university I was employed, and this was my first big achievement. Initially, I sent my Curriculum Vitae to a company because I wanted to test my ability. The company offered me a position as a part-time sales person after passing two stages of job interviews. I had a lot of hands-on experience when I decided to upgrade my knowledge by enrolling in a Nano Degree Digital Marketing Program. I successfully completed the program and immediately started putting all my knowledge into practice. It was an uphill task in the beginning, but now, as I give 100%, my progress is so satisfying. Now I have become more focused on self-development and am acquiring new skills every year. No matter how old I am, it will never be too late to keep learning because I want to become smarter and bolder.

Apart from my academics, I was also a volunteer for a local Non-Governmental Organization within South Sudan which worked toward ending child marriages and gender-based violence. We visited local orphanages and old-age homes to distribute food, clothes and other necessary items. Those were the best times of the week for me since I always looked forward to cheering up small children. It was a treat to watch them smile when they received items from us.

When I am not working, I spend my time in fulfilling and relaxing pursuits such as reading, cooking, listening to podcasts and music. I enjoy reading all kinds of books, but my favorites are those that portray the lives of soldiers during wartime or of big, complicated familial issues. Music and dance are calming and soothing. I love deep talks, travel and exploring life. The mantras I live by are: Always place my dignity at the top and always be kind. Once I was in need and I know the feelings of being without, so I am kind and want to help others in need. We don't know how much a small act of kindness means to someone in need. Long after all your material achievements are forgotten, your kindness lives on. A little empathy goes a long way.

For me to live a fulfilled life is my goal and every action of mine is a step toward it. The way I choose to live my life will decide how I achieve my

goal, and today I'm 1000 times better than I used to be. I am resolved that in the coming years I will be a successful CEO and a multi-challenge maker empowering fellow young women; impacting their lives positively by helping those in need and those who cannot support themselves financially. Most importantly, I wish to make South Sudan better than it is now since it is still a young country and the government is still trying to establish the infrastructure.

Other than that, I want to live an ordinary but beautiful life, enjoying each and every moment. I enjoy connecting with people and I am open to interesting work offers from clients within South Sudan and abroad, so send me an email akonesther9498@gmail.com and we can take it from there.

My advice: Whatever you do, put God first for He is the beginning and the end of our existence. You will not live forever. Make sure that you value each day that you are alive. Be in a hurry to do good. Pursue your dreams and aim for true happiness in every relationship you have by bringing out the best in every person. Look for purpose. Make the most out of today for it is a gift, that is why it is called the present. Yesterday is gone and tomorrow may never come. God bless you in your journey.

A Dinka Man's Fight for the Existence of his Language Abroad

By Tearz Ayuen/Africa World Books

Scholars argue that language is a part of culture. Through it, one is able to express cultural beliefs and values. Therefore, to teach someone your language is to teach them your culture as well.

Today, languages such as English, French, and Arabic are some of the major foreign languages taught and spoken in most African countries.

In some countries like Kenya, teachers force young schoolchildren to wear an animal bone around their necks during a lesson or break time as a punishment for uttering a non-English word in class.

And with the cultural globalization - the process through which the culture of one country or society is spread to other countries - storms taking over the whole world, several African observers have expressed fears of extinction of African languages and cultures.

One man, who envisages a possible total annihilation of one of the Sub-saharan African languages - The Dinka - if nothing is done right now to avert the lingual catastrophe, has embarked on writing folktales in Dinka.

"One of the greatest tools of influence is language. Today, Pop culture is killing other languages," says Manyang Deng.

A Nilotic language spoken in South Sudan, with over 4.5 million speakers, according to Indiana University and University of Cambridge, Dinka is an oral culture and became codified through the Arabic and Latin scripts during the late nineteenth and early twentieth centuries.

However, this was the work of outsiders, mostly missionaries, who translated the Bible in an attempt to spread the gospel in the Dinka society.

During the civil wars in the Sudan, especially the 21-year civil war (1983-2005), the Sudan Armed Forces - in its attempts to suppress rebellion led by Dr John Garang de Mabior - bombed civilian areas, including villages and cattle camps, claiming about two million lives and displacing four million people.

Hundreds of thousands of Dinka people fled to neighboring countries such as Kenya, Uganda, and Egypt, where some of them later had opportunities to resettle in the West.

Deng happens to be one of them. He relocated to the US in the early 2000s. Later on, he moved

to Australia, where he got married and is now raising a young family.

"I am afraid, our children are getting lost because there are no written materials for Dinka language and culture," the father of seven goes on to say.

Australia is a second home to tens of thousands of South Sudanese. Majority of them relocated to the continent in the 1990s and 2000s as children and adults; others were born there.

Though Australia is a multicultural country, which allows its citizens to practice their own cultures, Deng believes that the Australian-born Dinka are the ones at risk of disappearing into the pop culture wilderness. For good.

To help keep the culture alive, the father has written about eight books in the Dinka language. One of the books is ɣɔn në roor de cuɔl akɔl or Once Upon a Time in the Jungle of Sunset. Published in 2020, folktale contains 39 traditional fictional stories.

"My children struggle to speak Dinka. What then happens tomorrow to their children - my grandchildren?" He wonders. "The books I am writing are a preservation of our language, for generations to come."

Another interesting book under Deng's belt is the one on Dinka alphabets, which is said to be the first of its kind. Pïööc de Akeer ke Thoŋ de Jiëëŋ: Learning of the Dinka's alphabets.

The uniqueness of the English grammar book is the fact that it comprehensively explores the 33 Dinka alphabets. The author adequately examines each letter to ensure meaningful understanding.

It is designed to help a learner to learn quickly and with ease and be able to speak Dinka language fluently.

The South Sudan Transitional constitution recognizes all languages. However, none is taught at any school today. English is the official language, followed by Arabic.

Deng believes that South Sudan, a culturally and ethnically diverse country, will be a better place tomorrow when the local languages, about 64, are incorporated into the school curricula.

"A better South Sudan is a South Sudan where a Dinka child will be willing to learn Madi, Nuer, Acholi, or Bari language in school," he adds.

Some African cultures and languages that did not have a Deng and have died natural deaths include Mesmes and Weyto in Ethiopia, Kore in Kenya, Nyang'i and Singa in Uganda, Baygo and Torona in Sudan, Ngbee in DR Congo, and Horo and Muskum in Chad.

Why the Kiir administration Should Tap into South Sudanese Diaspora's Expertise

By Tearz Ayuen/Africa World Books

All over the world, a diaspora plays a key role in the economic development of its motherland. They are accredited for the economic boom in some countries, including Israel, Singapore, Bosnia, and Brazil.

These are all countries which experienced sorts of displacements - wars, civil wars, economic recessions and inflations.

After restoration of stability, many returned home to promote trade and foreign direct investment, create businesses and spur entrepreneurship, and transfer new knowledge and skills.

Today, South Sudanese diaspora in Australia have been calling upon the Kiir administration to adopt a policy that will help the government tap into its sea of skilled workforce.

There are roughly 20,000 South Sudanese citizens in Australia, thousands of whom have acquired "transferrable skills" and are currently working in both private and public sectors in the country.

As of today, the diaspora boasts of world class professionals, including surgeons, civil engineers, lawyers, academics, and bureaucrats.

But since the inception of the government of South Sudan in 2005, the leadership has been depending on the region for expertises. Kenyan and Ugandan nationals work in various sectors as experts, especially capacity building.

"Instead of paying foreign experts and specialists who drain the economy as they shift the cash outside the country, South Sudan has many opportunities to leverage the skills and expertise of her citizens in the diaspora and within," writes Akuot Aciek, president of South Sudan Community Association of Western Australia, in an open letter addressed to President Salva Kiir.

He argues that the government has every right, "with policies and proper engagement" to find a way to involve the diaspora in the development of the nascent country.

He states: "Transnational citizens can be active actors in nation-building as demonstrated by the government of Ghana, which has attracted more than 20,000 health professionals from the diaspora."

Recently, the Ghanaian government initiated a diaspora engagement program aimed at enhancing the capacity of Ghanaians abroad in a bid to effectively participate in national development in structured ways.

This was done through the channeling of their remittances to foster entrepreneurship, support innovation, and develop priority sectors of the economy.

In addition, the government believed that the diaspora could advance development agenda

through the use of their knowledge and skills to fill resources and knowledge gaps, as partners, and also as members and leaders of scientific and technical networks in Ghana.

Akuot says this is replicable, given the fact that South Sudan has a huge diaspora around the world, notably in the US, and Canada, needless to mention Australia.

Connecting with diasporas, and leveraging their various resources for development, the International Organization for Migration says it involves a multitude of government departments and other partners, and the interest and commitment of government at the highest levels to move such a cross-cutting agenda forward.

Observers noted that a governmental ministry or entity dedicated to diaspora issues could facilitate the necessary inter-ministerial coordination and ensure that these communities abroad are included in any national development plan.

Ghana and Kenya, for instance, have already established units within their respective governments to oversee diaspora affairs. Headed up by Alfred Mutua, the Ruto administration recently established the Ministry of Foreign and Diaspora Affairs, tasked with projecting, promoting and protecting Kenya's interests and image globally through innovative diplomacy, and contributing towards a just, peaceful and equitable world.

"Thus, South Sudan can strengthen its institutions, improves service delivery, develops its natural resources and stirs up its economic development by using her diaspora population that has enormous potential in helping the country in the following areas," argues Akuot, who is an economist by training.

Apart from lending Juba skills, the professionals outside South Sudan could also help champion foreign policies.

Currently, the Kiir administration suffers a number of problems related to lack of foreign policies and backup mechanisms.

For example, South Sudan is suffering financial sanctions and arms embargo the UN Security Council and Troika have put on it and some of Kiir's inner circle members like Vice President Taban Deng and Benjamin Bol Mel, presidential advisor on special programs.

"Therefore, South Sudanese here in the diaspora could be strong advocates and lobbyists for the interests of South Sudan if the government of South Sudan and South Sudanese communities in the diaspora have trusted and working communication channels and partnerships through the office's ambassadors in the western countries and charitable Organizations," he continues.

The diaspora in Australia goes on to remind the government that it has actually been helping citizens back home through upkeeps.

Akuot says though they remit money to individual families, such support in a way prevents people from taking to the streets to demand regime change.

"Such direct support provided by the diaspora has undoubtedly shielded the Government of South Sudan from civil disobedience that could have occurred from the cost of living pressures as the economy was decimated by war," adds the member of the Economic Society of Australia.

My Culture is My Identity

The story of a Kenyan-born,
Australian-raised South Sudanese girl
by Africa World Books

Maria Nyanhial Maker is from Rumbek, South Sudan. She was born in Kenya and migrated to Perth, Western Australia, in 2003 when had just turned 10 years of age 4 days before her arrival. She migrated with her 4 siblings and her mother.

Maria studied from primary to college in the new home. She multi-tasked, working at Commonwealth Bank as her first job, studying and making music as her hobby.

"Regardless of all that, I never forgot to get involved in my own cultural activities where I studied to read and write Dinka from my uncle Eli Magok Manyol and my Pastor Mathew Mading Malok," she writes in an email.

Nyanhial, also known as Agut-Yom, is a Mother, a Wife, a Dinka dialogue children's Author, a pathologist (phlebotomist), a community Disability Nursing Assistant, a business owner, an entrepreneur, an artist, a sports coordinator, coach and a secretary in the office of Rumbek Women Association in Western Australia.

Being born outside South Sudan, one would imagine less knowledge and interests in the South Sudanese culture and lifestyle. However, Agut-Yom grew up involving herself in her community, allowing herself to become 'nyan Muonyjang' (Dinka girl), unapologetically.

"I had a choice of choosing the Western way of life. But because I had great role models and strong beliefs, I chose to flourish as Nyan Jieng," she explains.

Agut-Yom is a name given to those who are brave enough to impale a cow and are respected for it in the Dinka culture.

Nyanhial heard about this. Once again, she was proud of this and needed to earn the respect of those back home who call people in the Western world "Athumaa", meaning someone who lacks knowledge of their culture.

Nyanhial certainly proved them wrong. She was physically unable to ceremoniously transfix a cow as she resides in Australia, but her husband sent money to buy the cow colored (Yom) for her to spear via Bluetooth (funny but true) with the help of their family members. Her generation had no interest in this but now, she has their attention.

In her view, culture is a very broad concept

which encompasses the norms, values, customs, traditions, habits, skills, knowledge, beliefs and the whole way of life of a group of people.

To a large degree, Agut-Yom argues, culture determines how members of society think and feel: it directs their actions and defines their outlook on life.

Culture defines accepted ways of behaving for members of society from that particular group. The Dinka community have vast cultural beliefs that make them who they are as a people.

"From a long list, I will name a few I adapted from my mother. They are: respect. Culturally respecting your elders, your community, family and yourself is one of the main practices that defines you as a good person," she outlines.

She recognizes traditional dances; she says her mother Regina Diing Manyol has always been an icon with a voice of an angel. She leads many groups in singing and dancing showcasing their music and dances from Rumbek at the age of 5 to her teenage years, in Kenya as a married woman, and in Australia where she leads in Western Australia.

"I was blessed with my mother's talent, beginning her dancing as a leader at Red Cross Catholic Church at Kakuma Refugee Camp at the age of 3 and in Australia where I was always put on the spotlight to lead due to my enthusiastic, energetic, and charismatic leadership," Agut-Yom narrates.

She grew to become one of the youth leaders in her community to lead the next generation before she was married.

As of now, Nyanhial is married to a Dinka man from Rumbek - Dock Meen Malak, with whom they have three beautiful children.

"We both are proud Dinka people and

culture," the happy young cultural enthusiast says.

Nyanhial Maker challenges all of the youth and the next generation who are getting lost, forgetting their cultures and traditions to re-think the struggles their parents and the last generations endured to bring them here for their betterment.

Relocating to a different country is great. There are many positive and negative factors that we as people face, she believes.

Nyanhial asks her peers whether to adapt to the negatives or the positives. As South Sudanese, she continues, what change will you take back home if you forget your footsteps?

"Who will you be when you return to your motherland? Will you be a role model to the next generation?" she asks.

"Your culture is your identity. Without it, you are a lost sheep with no herd and no home to return to."

Back to his Roots

by William Mayom

The gentleman in these photos is Atem Bior Atem, famously known by his oxen name, "Atem Aduldul". But don't let his traditional attire fool you. Atem Bior is a great veteran; he was my battalion mate during the liberation struggle of the SPLA. He was famously known as Atem Fanan, because he was a composer and the lead singer of the First Battalion of the Red Army of Zalzal Two Division of the SPLA. Comrade Atem Bior was among the first Red Army forces discharged from Dimma and sent to help liberate the Equatoria region in 1988.

Comrade Atem Bior composed many famous revolutionary songs, which aroused emotional and cognitive responses that shaped and altered the experiences of the Red Army fighters. During the training and exercise, Atem's songs generated beneficial physical and emotional responses, creating a sense of synchronicity and cohesion and instigating zeal and bravery in the Red Army fighters. Remember, revolutionary songs as part of military activity not only helped to generate eagerness in the fighters but also directly contributed to the triggering of beneficial physical and psychological responses. Hence, songs were intrinsic to drill exercise, and joint singing unified soldiers in physical expression and ideology to persevere, endure hardships, and fight adamantly. Through songs, Comrade Atem attempted to promote mental, moral, and physical manhood in the fighters, increase their combat efficiency, and regulate the soldiers' emotions in line with their revolutionary duties. The following is one of the revolutionary songs Atem composed:

When the Red Army of Gredal is discharged,
we will capture Sadiq;
The bourgeoisie {will be kicked} out,
and Dr. John {will be installed} in;
The Red Army of John is coming,
You better respect us in Sudan,
you uncivilized Sadiq el Mahdi,
Sadiq and Suara Dahab will be banned,
The old Sudan will be demolished,
As declared by Dr. Garang,
New Sudan will be captured by Kalashnikov of the Red Army of Gredall!

Comrade Atem's songs were not just about artistic innovations but about songs that evoked bravery, combat, and rebellion. What made Comrade Atem unique was his deep thunderous voice, complimented by his Dinka Twii accent. While sitting in the parade ground situated in the mountainous part of Ethiopia to sing our revolutionary song, our lead singer, Atem Fanan, would send his deep, croaky voice, waking every living creature would be awake. The morale songs composed by Comrade Atem were very powerful and they determined the high spirit of the soldiers. The following is such a song:

You Sadiq el Mahdi
Sudan is our country
Dr. Garang is our president
Our land is being messed up by the bourgeoisie
That we don't know the situation of our country.
Ya Dr. Garang, bring Kalashnikov to the Red Army of Gredall
Sadiq will run!

To this day, many Red Army veterans still remembered quite a number of Atem's songs even 36 years after they were composed.

After getting the job done (liberating the country), Comrade Atem has transitioned from the military back to his traditional root. Currently, he is one of the famous artists who produced many albums using modern musical equipment. You will find many of his songs on YouTube. Comrade Atem is a devoted traditionalist who takes pride in his culture and traditions. As a proud member of his ethnicity, Twii, Comrade Atem is spreading cultural understanding to the community through leadership, willpower, devotion, and enthusiasm. For instance, Atem acquired his song ox, (picture attached), according to Comrade Reuben Mayen Garang. After the acquisition of his magnificent beast, Atem's clansmen welcomed and blessed the ox by killing one hundred cows. This honor killing of cattle is known as "rioŋ", "biɔl" or "buɔl" in Dinka dialects.

While there are fake veterans who are arrogantly displaying ranks claiming to be generals, though they had not even seen, let alone attended, a training center of the SPLA, veterans like Comrade Atem are quiet and humbled, downplaying their achievements. Comrade Atem is one of the veterans who has successfully transitioned from the military back to his cultural roots.

The author, William Mayom, who lives in Canada, can be reached at willymayom@yahoo.ca He is the author of two books, *The Proud People* and *Learning the Heard Way*

TWIC East Leaders in Australia Encourage Children to Learn Dinka Language, Help Mangalla IDPs Return Home

By Tearz Ayuen/Africa World Books

The third annual general meeting of the Twic East Community Association of Australia (TECAA) has concluded, with several resolutions, including calls for the need to teach children in the Dinka language.

Held in Canberra on 8-9 April, the two-day event brought together high-level officials of the association, prominent Twic East community leaders from Africa, and invited guests representing Twic East neighbors in South Sudan.

Among the officials were TECAA President Mamer Yaak Dut, His Deputy Mabior Mabil Atem, Secretary General Makuach Mabior Deng, the entire executive body, advisors, Council of Elders, Youth and Women leaders, formers leaders, state/territory leaders, payam leaders, local Twi organizations, and neighbors from Duk, Bor, and other Dinka guests representing their communities in Canberra.

The Annual general meeting resolved around three main issues, namely: A need for teaching children in Dinka language, help settle the displaced residents of Twic East who are currently in Mangalla in Central Equatoria and a review of the association's constitution.

THE DINKA LANGUAGE CONCERN

Reports show that drought, famine, and war resulted in large numbers of Sudan-born and South Sudan-born refugees leaving for neighboring countries like Kenya and Egypt, and many were later resettled in Australia.

Australia is a vibrant, multicultural country. It is home to the world's oldest continuous cultures, as well as Australians who identify with more than 270 ancestries, according to the Australian Human Rights Commission.

"Learning the Dinka language will contribute some important means of understanding the cultural aspects and history in order to participate in multilingual societies at home and here in Australia," Anyieth Duom, TECAA's information secretary, told Ramciel Magazine.

Since 1945, it says almost seven million people have migrated to Australia. This rich, cultural diversity is one of our greatest strengths.

The 2021 Australian census recorded 8,255 people born in South Sudan. 14,273 people, however, indicated that they had South Sudanese ancestry.

The Twic community statistics and population stands at 5,548. Out of this number, 3,066 are below the age of 18.

"This interaction develops the disposition to explore the perspectives behind the Dinka traditional heritage and practices of cultures in order to value such intercultural experiences," Duom continued.

Duom's argument is backed up by the United Nations Educational, Scientific and Cultural Organization (UNESCO) research, which indicates that education in the mother tongue is a key fac-

tor for inclusion and quality learning, and it also improves learning outcomes and academic performance.

It argues that this is crucial, especially in primary school to avoid knowledge gaps and increase the speed of learning and comprehension.

RESETTLEMENT OF IDPS

In 2020, thousands of people fled their homes with few or no belongings when floods submerged parts of South Sudan, especially in Jonglei State in Twic East, Bor, and Duk counties.

Many sought refuge at an Internally Displaced Persons (IDP) camp in Mangalla, Central Equatoria state.

In May 2022, the most recent statistics available, 38,658 IDPs were living in this area that was established in June 2020, including 2,466 children below the age of five.

After flood waters subsided, those from Bor County returned to their respective homes, leaving IDPs from Twic East since they have nothing to back home to after the flooding completely destroyed homes.

With the support from humanitarian groups, UN agencies and the national and state governments, the vulnerable people are expected to be repatriated to Twic East sometime later this year or so.

"Twi East Community Association of Australia (TECAA) is a member of Twic East Global Table that includes Twi East Community Association--USA and Twi East Community Association of Canada," Duom explained.

"These groups are prepared to help with health care and education when the repatriation process takes place."

TECAA CONSTITUTIONAL REVIEW

Established in 2008, TECAA has been the umbrella leadership of every Twic East indegene in Australia, dealing with matters that concern its members.

However, the association has been led by males since its inception. Its first president was Yaak Deng Akoy, followed by Mangar Ayuel Malual, Kuer Dau Apai in 2016, Deng Chol Riak in December 2018 and now Mamer Yaak Dut, the incumbent.

In the April annual general assembly, some members raised concern over the male dominance, with some suggesting a sister association for women.

"The only striking issue was whether the Twic East Community Association of Australia (TECAA) needed to have a separate independent women association to run concurrently with the existing organization," Duom recalled.

This, he said, prompted the association to agree to review the constitution in order to accommodate new ideas that could help solve new problems.

"TECAA's constitution is a progressive document that is regularly reviewed or checked to meet the demands and needs. The review process is triggered when there are emerging concerns that threaten or undermine the progress of the organization," Duom explained.

He added that the meeting transferred the matter to the states assemblies to conduct a referendum on whether to "uphold the current article or to change it".

Also in attendance were 10 prominent Twic leaders from Africa, including Hon.Biar Mading Biar, Deputy Chair of TECA-Juba, the former State Minister of Land and Housing (Jonglei State) and guest of honor of the event, Hon. Deng Mabeny Kuot, Commissioner of Twic East County Hon. Dau Akoi Jurkuch, former commissioner of Twic East County, and the Chairperson of Mangala IDPs, Bishop Dr. Isaiah Majok Dau.

Others were, Dr Bishop Isaiah Majok Dau,- the former General Oversee of Sudan Pentecostal Churches and the current peace advocate and facilitator and invited speaker on peace and harmony; Rt Rev. Abraham Duot Kuer, the Diocesan Bishop of Jonglei Province - Anglican Church of South Sudan; Rev. Canon Mary Achol Deng-Nuer, Rev. Canon Jacob Deng Manyang, Jacob Manyuon Deng, Abraham Chol Riak, Atem Akuoch Miot, Sultan Atem Maguong Ayii Kuol, and Joseph Garang Deng.

Aduk Gideon Dau
The Jonglei daughter educating vulnerable children in Kenya

By Tearz Ayuen

Assume you're stranded in a desert, Sahara's in particular. Every foodstuff you had is getting depleted. Food is rotting. Bread is drying up, almost into a stone. Water is scarce.

Your toes are peeping through holes of a worn out pair of Nike sneakers; lips are cracked. The scorching sun is barbecuing your skin, which is beginning to smell like a poorly cooked dried fish from Dhiam-dhiam.

With you are tens of thousands of people, who are desperate as you are. Luckily enough, a helicopter suddenly comes from nowhere. However, you're the only one who gets picked and airlifted to safety. What then would you do about the people you left?

Ok. Wait. What if you were under similar circumstances, but different setting, say, at Kakuma Refugee Camp in northern Kenya? But now the situation is real and it is the 1990s. However, you are not the one in trouble this time round. It is Aduk Gideon Dau.

Established in 1992, especially to host the then Southern Sudanese, who had fled the civil war, the living conditions at the camp became unbearable.

Families depended on food rations distributed by the United Nations agencies, mostly the World Food Program and other international church organizations such as the Lutheran World Federation.

The food ration included a kilogram of maize grains, a 250-milliliter tin of oil, spoonful of salt, and 300-gram tin of lentils that was expected to last 14 days before the next food distribution day. The food was ever inadequate. But wise men say half a loaf is better than no bread at all. Life went on.

Seven years after subsisting on the aforementioned foodstuffs at the camp, Aduk Gideon Dau and her family grabbed an opportunity to resettle in Sydney in New South Wales, Australia - a near--heaven. Literally.

It was characterized by good feeding. Good health. And a fountain of opportunities to lead a better life. Her children went to a good school. Hunger became a thing of the past.

One day, she thought about the camp and the families who remained behind. "I have everything now. I eat good food; sleep in a good house, on a good bed. What do I do to help them?" Aduk thought to herself.

Later on, 'Education is key' hit her. As a result, she gathered friends, members of the community and church to pool resources in order to actualize the idea.

These include disadvantaged learners who garner good marks in the Kenya Certificate of Primary Education examinations, those being raised by single parents, mostly women, and the ones without any parent - orphans.

"And because sometimes determination to pursue education differs among individuals, we also look for those who have the will to take the scholarship seriously," Aduk explained.

The scholarships fund four years of secondary education for each recipient, with a year's fees costing $1800. The recipients of the scholarships live as boarders in one of a handful of schools chosen for their Christian ethos, cost, proximity to the

"The best way I could give back to our Jonglei community is to help educate less fortunate children," said Aduk, a nurse by profession.

In 2017, she founded the Lost Children of Jonglei Scholarships to educate clever but less fortunate children at the camp, whose learning services have deteriorated over the years due to shortages of funds.

Every year, the foundation - hugely supported by the Anglican Aid - has two slots for best performers - a girl and a boy. And because there are so many children in need, there are criteria that a child who wishes to be sponsored must meet.

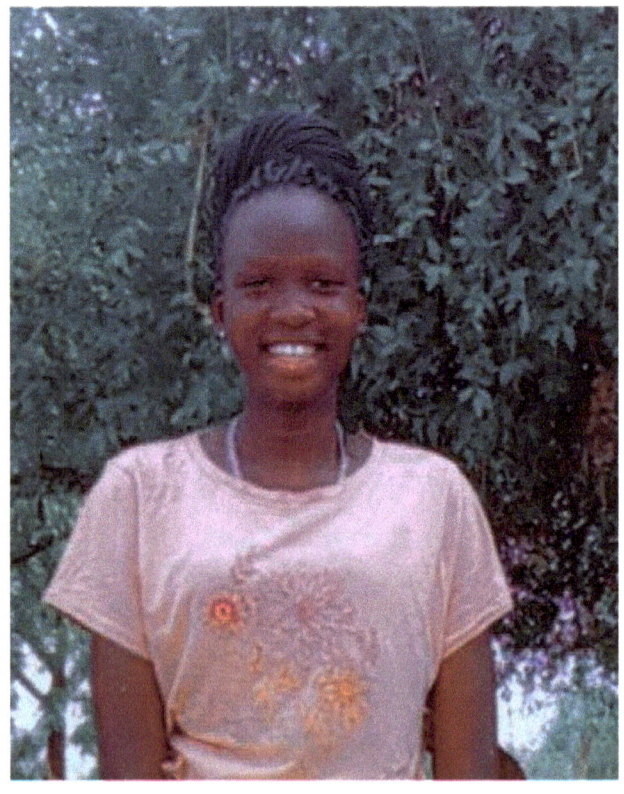

refugee camp, and availability of places in Form 1.

Because the project is dependent on well--wishers or people of goodwill, a sponsor commits to supporting one student during the four years of high school, or they donate any amount towards the general scholarship fund.

So far, the first batch graduated recently. Adhieu Majok Chuol and Garang Anyuon Manyuon performed well in the Kenya Certificate of Secondary Education, with both scoring mean grade B+.

If she gets lucky to land another scholarship, Adhieu says she would like to enroll for a Bachelor of Science (BSc) in Petroleum Engineering.

"I know the seekers were many but I was lucky to be among the chosen ones. It is through this scholarship that my education at Moi Girls - Nangili was comfortable," an elated Adhieu explained.

"I would like to give back to society by taking a course in Petroleum Engineering."

For his part, Garang says he is into the health sector. Back home in Jonglei and South Sudan in general, the health situation is dire due to lack of skilled health professionals, several reports show.

To contribute to the improvement of the sector, Garang says he is interested in pursuing a course in Nursing.

"I do hope that I will honor the scholarship in all my pursuits, including furthering my education and helping vulnerable people in the whole of South Sudan," he said from Kakuma.

Aduk, who has dedicated a day among the five working days to woo potential sponsors, called upon the government of South Sudan to help her scholars

"I would like the concerned government institutions to pick up from where I stop by offering the children scholarships at the University of Juba," said Aduk.

As of April 30, 2022, a total of 182,6351 people, mostly South Sudanese refugees, resided in Kakuma refugee camps (Kakuma 1, Kakuma 2, Kakuma 3, and Kakuma 4 camps), according to UNHCR.

Thousands of the families there are believed to be from Jonglei State. The founder also appealed to sons and daughters to help whenever they can those in need.

"We are all burdened with the responsibility of helping those in need. Let's elevate each other. Even a dollar counts," she added.

Twic East Community Leaders doing wonders in Western Australia

By Tearz Ayuen, Nairobi

Due to several civil wars in Sudan, particularly the 21-year liberation struggle which ended in 2005, many South Sudanese have found themselves in distant foreign lands. These include the Americas, Europe, and Australia.

Some arrived in the foreign cities with their families - spouses and young children. Others resettled as young unmarried.

A multicultural society, South Sudanese communities - through associations - are also trying their best to find their rightful places on the continent.

In Western Australia - a subdivision that is larger than some of the biggest countries in Africa, notably DR Congo or Algeria, a South Sudanese community association is helping promote multiculturalism in the country.

This is none other than Twic East Community Association in Western Australia (TECAWA) - an officially registered community organization based in Perth.

"The organization has over ten years in providing services to the Twic East community and general South Sudanese in Western Australia," says Chol Riek Garang, TECAWA president.

He explains that one of the core objectives of the association is to provide a forum on which members interact, exchange and discuss economic, social and cultural issues of concerns and find solutions for the advancement of the community.

With children born into a culture different from their parents', some of them find themselves on the wrong side of the law.

Others, after graduating from high school, find

CHOL RIEK GARANG, PRESIDENT

it difficult to choose a career to pursue at the higher learning institutions.

To help such young people, TECAWA has come up with Year 12 Celebrations, an initiative that brings together graduates whereby they are addressed by important figures in the community, including doctors, lawyers, and engineers.

"During the Year 12 Celebrations, the invited professionals inspire the youth in an attempt to help them achieve the Australia dream," Riek told Ramciel Magazine.

In addition, there have been media reports suggesting juvenile crimes among the South Sudanese community in Australia.

Though crime incidents are uncommon in Western Australia, TECAWA's objective is to prevent such from happening.

All these years, the association has been hiring public spaces such as sports centers and gardens to carry out its functions.

However, this will soon change after the community raised a lot of money for building a cultural center.

"We raised a good amount of money. But because the land is expensive, we are in communication with a bank to help us actualize the dream," Riek continued.

A beehive of activities, the TECAWA Center will be hosting traditional dances, weddings, community meetings, and many more.

The association also prides itself in its contributions to the fight against the Covid-19 pandemic.

When the pandemic hit Australia, the association leadership quickly set up committees tasked with specific roles to ensure that every community member was well-informed of the dangers of the virus and what one could do whenever they developed symptoms.

"We acted as a backup to the state health authorities. And as a result of our joint efforts, we all survived the Coronavirus. No lives were lost during the two-year period," said the father of two.

TECAWA has several other objectives, including:

- To develop, promote, and foster community spirit, cultural heritage, unity, trust and social values of the community;
- To liaise with government agencies, departments, and non-governmental organizations to assist in integrating newly-arrived immigrants or refugees into Western Australia;
- To encourage and engage youth to promote Twic East Community social and cultural activities;
- To promote multiculturalism, social service and cultural exchange with other communities, associations, charities or organizations;
- To empower and encourage girls and women to participate in employment or microenterprises; and to organize and celebrate community events or festivals and share positive socio-economic contributions of Twic East with other wider Australian communities in Western Australia.

RAMCIEL

BOOK REVIEW

It is extraordinary how life works - the obstacles a child can overcome – the way our lives can intersect.

I met Deng Atem thirty years ago in a refugee camp in northern Kenya called Kakuma. I was twenty-five years old and just starting out as a reporter, shooting, writing and producing stories for an educational newscast called Channel One.

I had just returned to Kenya from Baidoa, Somalia, a town hit hard by famine and fighting, when I read about large numbers of children and teenagers, who'd escaped war in Sudan and were now at Kakuma.

Deng was about thirteen or fourteen years old when I met him. He spent most of the day I was there with another reporter who was visiting the camp, a Danish journalist named Jesper Strudsholm, but Deng is the kind of person who leaves a lasting impression.

Kakuma was the first refugee camp I ever visited, and it was immediately clear there was a lot more going on there than any of the Sudanese young people were willing or able to talk about. It was also quite clear the kids had been coached. As Deng writes in this stirring and heartfelt memoir, he and the others had been given instructions by their elders about what they should say to reporters.

Deng was told to use his baptismal name, Moses, to emphasize he and the others were Christians being persecuted by the Islamic government in Sudan, and he writes, they were told not to let anyone know they had been trained to fight. When I met him, Deng now writes, he had already taken part in one battle and had been present at a second.

At night, we all came together for some traditional dancing. While most of the kids seemed excited to take part in the festivities, I remember Deng was more interested in trying out my video camera, which I was happy to let him use. When I left the next day, I couldn't help but worry about

what would happen to him and all the young people I'd met who had already been through so much.

In 2018 I was in Phoenix, Arizona, speaking at ASU. When I got off the stage, I was handed a note that had been passed along by someone in the audience. It was a note from Deng. I couldn't believe it. He came backstage and we had a chance to reconnect and the memories of Kakuma came flooding back.

What an extraordinary story Deng has to tell! It is not just about South Sudan; it is a universal story about survival and determination - how a child can face the most difficult of situations and find a way through them. It is a privilege to introduce you to Deng Atem and his moving memoir, Jump the Ram.

~Anderson Cooper, CNN Anchor

Book Review

This book is an annotated collection of the many works of Dr Francis Mading Deng, South Sudan's most esteemed elder statesman, diplomat, academic and writer.

Son of a Ngok Dinka Paramount Chief, Dr Deng has had a remarkable 40-year career and the sheer quantity of writing that he has produced makes him one of Africa's most prolific writers.

In many ways this is a reference book; the rich pickings can be dipped into at random, it could be read cover to cover, or a reference can be located in the appendix which lists the writings by subject. Some of the annotations are brief and others very long, but all point to the full works of the author and other's writing in the field. The vast number of titles are organised under the central themes of identity, dignity, diversity and equality, within four interconnected levels: local, national, regional and global.

"The significance of listing my works under levels is to emphasize the element of continuity and interconnectedness in change reflected at the various phases or levels of my journey through cultures. The local level is where I was born and raised. The national level comprises early education and later government service. The regional level covers my African continental perspective and engagement. And the global level includes graduate studies abroad and later research in think tanks and finally United Nations service from which I transitioned again to serve my new country of South Sudan as the first Permanent Representative to the United Nations."

This book is for anyone with an interest in Africa, South Sudan and in writing itself. Dr

Deng writes with great clarity and intellectual rigour, wisdom and insight, addressing a vast array of subjects, (a few of whichh are recurrent throughout). His exploration of identity is especially compelling.

"Very often, people take for granted what they are in terms of identity and related cultural values. In that condition, they may not be well equipped to transmit to their interlocutors in the cross-cultural context what they carry with them and contribute to the process of cross-cultural diffusion and enrichment. They need to read about themselves as much as others need to read about them."

www.ingramcontent.com/pod-product-compliance
Lightning Source LLC
Chambersburg PA
CBHW061536010526
44107CB00066B/2888